Genero

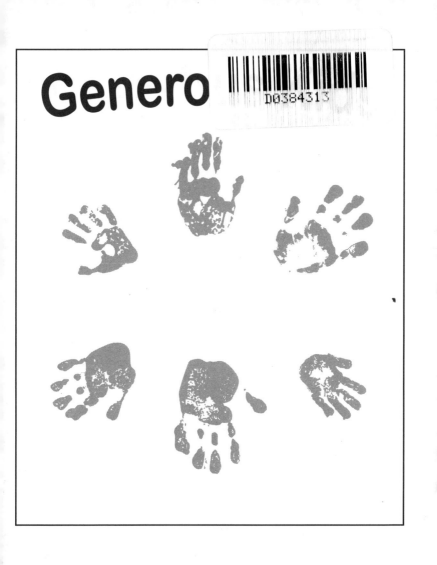

Generous Kids

Helping Your Child
Experience the Joy of Giving

Colleen O'Donnell & Lyn Baker

GENEROUS KIDS

Manufactured in the United States of America

For information, please contact:

Brown Books Publishing Group

16200 North Dallas Parkway, Suite 170

Dallas, Texas 75248

www.brownbooks.com

972-381-0009

A New Era in Publishing™

ISBN-13: 978-1-933285-96-2

ISBN-10: 1-933285-96-6

LCCN 2007931820

1 2 3 4 5 6 7 8 9 10

http://www.generouskids.com

The authors have designated 20 percent of profits from the sales of Generous Kids for children's charities.

All the names of the *Generous Kids* quoted have been changed to protect their privacy.

"No one has yet realized the wealth of sympathy, the kindness and generosity hidden in the soul of a child."

—*Emma Goldman*

Dedication

This book is dedicated to you, the adult, who has chosen this book with an eye toward improving the life of a child. Because you are reading this foreword, we already know a lot about you. You have a deep concern both for the well-being of young people and for the betterment of the world you live in.

Research shows that the simple act of teaching our children the habit of giving can change generations for good.

You have our heartfelt admiration and support. Visit our Web site for additional ideas on effecting positive change in our world through giving with intention and consistency.

http://www.generouskids.com

Chapters

"You get the best out of others when you give the best of yourself."

—*Harvey Firestone*

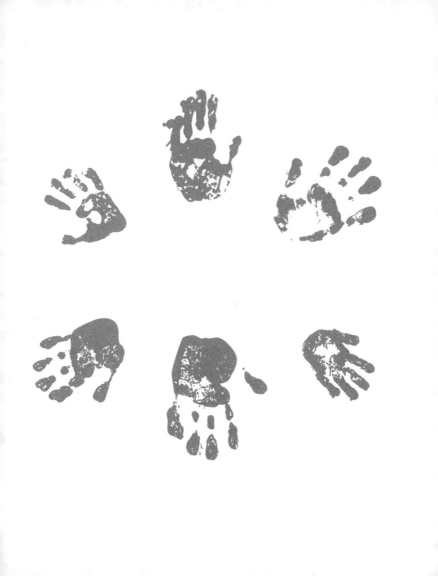

Giving on Purpose

How to expand your child's view of giving
and his experience of living!

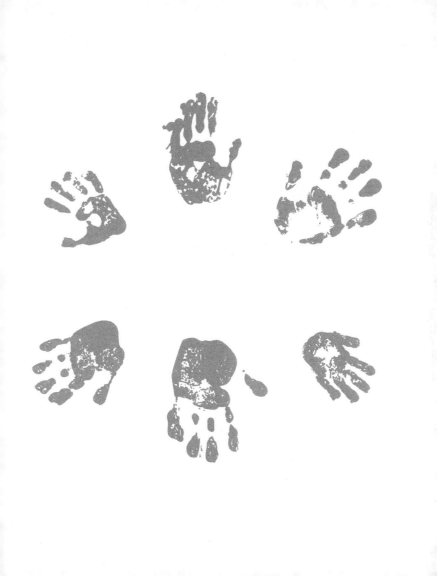

Chapter One

Let's Get Intentional about Giving

"We are what we repeatedly do; excellence then is not an act but a habit."

—*Aristotle*

Nobody likes to be around a selfish kid.

Let's face it. Every child, and that includes each one of us, comes right out of the factory with a selfish streak that just won't quit. It's human nature. One of the first words out of our mouths at about age two is: "Mine!" Unfortunately, this "*mine* set" follows many of us into adulthood. Fortunately, however, we are not completely selfish, for generosity is also very much a part of human nature. Our task as parents, then, is to bring out the hidden generosity of our children through good habits—both *our* habits and *theirs*.

So, how best can we teach giving? First, as parents, we need to practice what we preach. The fact that we don't is a big part of the problem. Recognizing this disconnect between our intentions and our actions, we become embarrassed, and instead of doing something about it, we feel guilty and get sidelined. Our crazy, busy lives distract us from the authentic joy that accompanies a lifestyle of giving.

Yet, genuine giving feels great, so why don't we do it? Perhaps we have forgotten what we learned as kids, or perhaps never learned. But then why don't children, unburdened by all those adult distractions, give more? Because we haven't reinforced that natural pleasure we all take in sharing. We haven't, in other words, taught them the HABIT of giving. Yes, that is correct. **Giving is a habit**, and we can teach our kids how to give just as we've taught them how to brush their teeth, make their beds, and say "please" and "thank you."

Whether we like it or not, much of what we do with our kids is "sell" them on doing things we believe are in their best interests. We "sell" them on eating their vegetables, washing their faces, saying their prayers, wearing a coat in the winter, and doing their homework. So why don't we "sell" them on giving? Just to make sure they would "buy" it, though, we first collected some data to see what kids thought about giving.

Chapter Two

The Giving Project

"It's important to talk to children about making giving a habit rather than an isolated holiday activity."

—*Dan Rice, World Vision*

After a tsunami hit Southeast Asia in December 2004, we overheard several high school students who had participated in various fundraisers talking about the money they had collected. Though they felt good about getting involved, they wondered whether or not it had really done any good. These were two typical comments: "We gave, but I doubt it made any difference," and "Yeah, it's like all the community service we do is just another homework assignment."

We were amazed, and wondered—do kids really "get" giving? So, we created and sent out a questionnaire, "The Giving Project," to approximately 1,000 students from three to twenty years old. We asked three questions of young people who were of various socioeconomic levels, different races, and a variety of religions:

What does giving mean to you?

Tell about a time when you gave and it made a difference.

Tell about a time when someone gave to you and it made a difference.

We noticed a couple things about their answers. There were some common misconceptions or misunderstandings evident in many of the answers, regardless of the kids' backgrounds. For example, many described giving as something we do for people whom we regard as "less" than we are.

Also, very few students viewed such activities as listening to a friend or helping their parent cook a meal or set the table as examples of giving. Quite a few examples, in fact, focused simply on giving money.

The lack of understanding of what giving is was displayed in the students' answers. Some of the answers startled us. Some kids couldn't remember a time when they had made a difference through their giving, and others were unable to recall a time when someone gave to them.

However, other answers were inspiring:

"I would say the best gift someone gave me was friendship."
Kay—age 19

"I gave two of my pink ponies to my friend. She liked this."
Elenora—age 3

"I've been told that laughter is the best medicine. And that's why, when my friend gave me the gift of laughter after I'd had a terrible day, I felt cured."
Chris—age 19

"I had quarters. My friend had one. I gave her two more. That made her happy."
Alex—age 6

"My friend gave me their jacket because I was cold; they knew how easily I get sick."
Chuck—age 14

We knew, based on our survey, that there was much work to do if the joy of giving was to be understood and applied in everyday living.

Chapter Three

Giving

"We make a living by what we get; we make a life by what we give."

—*Winston Churchill*

L istening to the voices of the children in The Giving Project, we composed a primer to address the essential ele-
ments of giving. We followed the example of many faith traditions and separated giving into three basic areas:

1) *Time*—The most precious of commodities; giving time
   as a gift sends the message: "You or this cause matter
   to me."

2) *Talent*—Abilities such as singing, woodworking, public speaking, sculpting, using a computer well, or playing the violin are all skills one has by endowment or
   effort; giving them as a gift sends the message: "I want
   to share my talents with the world."

3) *Treasure*—Usually this is money one has earned
   through hard work; giving it as a gift sends the message: "I believe in supporting your good works." We
   send this gift out into the world to share with others.

How can we make giving a regular act in our children's lives? The simpler, the better! By breaking down the concept of giving into three areas, we can easily help our kids make giving a simple and fulfilling habit—and a lot of fun. Time, Talent, and Treasure create the "Giving Circle."

The Giving Circle

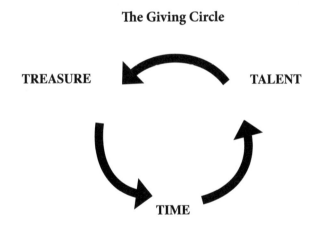

TREASURE

TALENT

TIME

You can enter the Giving Circle at any point and participate in a more abundant life!

Chapter Four

Kid-Giving and Kid-Character

"I have found that among its other benefits, giving liberates the soul of the giver."

—*Maya Angelou*

The impact that kid-giving has on kid-character is dramatic. When kids (and parents) get into giving, something amazing happens: *the giver's life is forever transformed in the process*. When a child makes giving a part of his or her life, he or she experiences three powerful effects:

1. A sense that when he gives to others, *he makes a difference.*

2. A greater appreciation and *gratitude for what she has* in her life.

3. A belief that being generous is a key to *personal happiness.*

This life transformation is most likely to happen, moreover, if giving begins at a young age. In 2002, an organization devoted to the study of philanthropy, called Independent

Sector, released the findings of their report, *Engaging Youth in Life Long Service*. Based on a national telephone survey of more than 4,000 adults, some of the significant findings of the study include the following:

- Forty-four percent of adults volunteer. Two-thirds of these adults began volunteering when they were young.

- Adults who began volunteering as youth are twice as likely to volunteer as those who did not start young.

- **Those who volunteered as young people and whose parents also volunteered became the most generous adults.**

Furthermore, research shows that there are personal benefits to young people who volunteer:

♦ They are **more likely to do well in school**.[1]

♦ They are **less likely to abuse alcohol/drugs**.[2]

♦ Volunteering **helps teens develop leadership skills** such as learning to respect others, developing patience, and having a better understanding of what makes a good citizen.[3]

Teach your children to give! Volunteer alongside them. Your child will benefit, your family will benefit, your community will benefit. It's a win-win-win outcome! It is one of the most important things we can do to help them grow up to be good people and to ensure that they will build a better future for all of us!

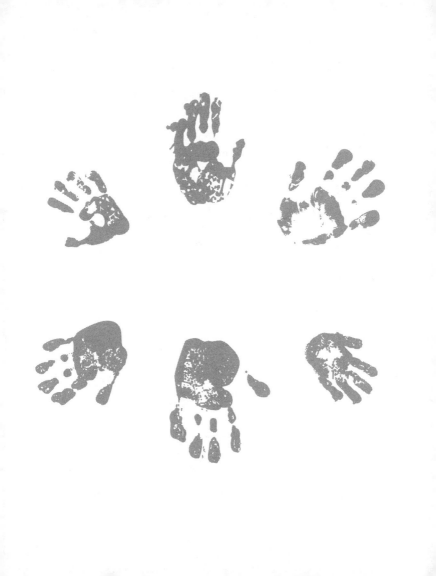

Chapter Five

Fascinating Facts
and Figures

"The habit of giving only enhances the desire to give."

—*Walt Whitman*

Giving builds more than just character; it helps build the community beyond the family, as well. The "private sector" of society plays a crucial role in maintaining and advancing our quality of life, but it also has a very practical financial impact.

- Independent Sector has calculated the value of a volunteer hour based on Bureau of Labor statistics. For the year 2005, the volunteer hour was calculated as being worth $18.04 per hour with a total economic value of $280 billion.[4]

- More than 1.3 billion hours of service were contributed in 2004 by 15.5 million youths between the ages of twelve and eighteen.[5]

- Charitable Giving reached an estimated $260.28 billion in 2005.[6]

- Young people who attended religious services were nearly twice as likely to be regular volunteers as young people who do not attend religious services at all.[7]

A new study released in 2005 by The Corporation for National and Community Service continued to find positive connections between volunteering and higher grades as well as stronger family ties. The data show the probability of a more active involvement in the community in his future when a child volunteers with his family.[8]

Chapter Six

Love Is a Four-Letter Word Spelled T.I.M.E.

What a child doesn't receive he can seldom later give."

—*P. D. James*

Our sons and daughters learn best when they see us in action. And lately, for many of us, what they've been seeing is that we are not in action enough.

One of the most meaningful things we can do is to give of our time. But how can we do this? We have work proposals to complete, ball games to attend, shopping to do, and schedules to meet. Is it any wonder that one of the simplest habits to teach our children—the giving of our time—is perhaps the hardest?

Love is spelled T.I.M.E.

T—Thankful

Doesn't it all start with being thankful? Wherever we are in life, it could be worse (we know, we've been there) or it could be better. Being thankful right where we stand always empowers us to do and be more; it lightens our load and reminds us how blessed we are. Grace has been said at dinner tables for generations to remind us all of what we truly have. Instilling this thankfulness in our children begins (once again) with us. Cultivate the attitude of gratitude with your kids!

I—Intentional

Become intentional about your giving. In order to make giving a habit, we must schedule our time to give just as we do a doctor's appointment, working out at the gym, or our vacation. We all can find thirty minutes each week to spend time with our children in an *intentional* act of giving. This helps create the habit. Whether it's stuffing bulletins for the local YMCA or visiting a sick friend, pulling weeds at the nearby park or going to the SPCA to play with the animals, we can find time in our schedule to create the habit of giving when it is important to us. So open your calendars now and make a rendezvous with giving.

M—Message

Your commitment of time sends a clear message to your child that giving is important. This message becomes a part of who they are as an adult. Also, where you choose to spend your time sends a message about what and who is important to you and your family. Many a generous adult has thanked their parents publicly for "making them" go to sing at a nursing home, participate in a scout project, or pick up trash in a park (how many times did you need to hear, "Leave the place better than you found it?" before that message became a part of you?). Where else will our children learn this habit? The message of where you are spending your time is coming through loud and clear to your child—is it the message you want them to hear?

E—Easy

Intentionally creating the habit of giving is easy and fun. Spend time with your children conversing about giving and find out what is important to them. You may discover they have a special interest in The Little Red School House and making sure the birds are fed, going to breakfast with the neighbor who lost his wife, teaching guitar to someone who has never heard or seen a real musical instrument, or making cookies for their older brother or sister in college. Soon you'll see the thirty minutes per week you've been scheduling grow into an hour or more with ease.

Be **Thankful** (and share that with your children), be **Intentional** (put it in your schedule), send a clear **Message,** and remember, it's **Easy**!!

Kids Who Keep on Giving

Simple ways you can engage kids in giving
at each age and stage of their lives.

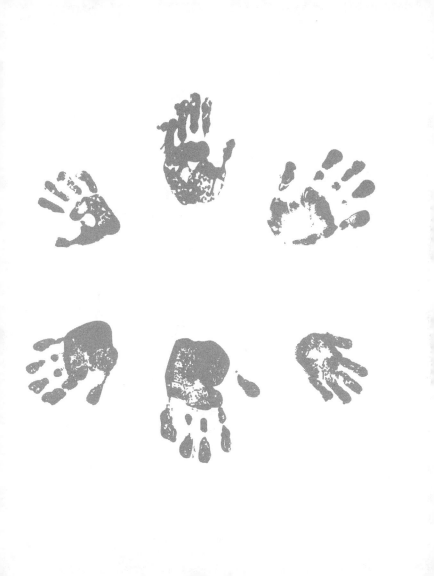

Chapter Seven

Start 'Em Early!

Ages 3-7

"Charity begins at home but should not end there."

—*Sir Francis Bacon*

Learning to give begins at home. That's why this is a book for parents. Teach the habit of giving in the same way you teach your young children to tie their shoes, pick up their toys, or wash their face.

If your child has had a stable, responsive home environment during his first three years of life, he is ready to test his competence and confidence in a slightly wider arena. "See what I did!" is the rallying cry of the early preschool years.

Children this age are concrete thinkers and drawn to hands-on experiences. They relate to their immediate community, family, or school environment. Most important to them is sharing something they have made themselves or collected from family and friends. Young children have no framework with which to make any sense of collecting money to give to strangers.

At home, start teaching them about giving and allow them the opportunity to put it into practice. Let them put the napkins on the table, feed the cat, and pick up their rooms. In school, let them decide what to bring to share with their class. Sharing simple things like crayons and toys at home is an elementary and powerful way to teach children to be generous from the beginning.

Encourage small acts of giving on a daily basis, and praise them for their contributions and efforts. Include them when you participate in a service project. This is a great way for your children to learn to help in a protected environment with you as the role model.

Read picture books about kindness and generosity. Talk about your family's giving traditions. Such stories will plant seeds of generosity and kindness in your children.

Movies with themes of giving and caring can have a powerful impact on your nonreader. We've chosen the books and movies in our resource section to help you begin this conversation with your young children.

If you establish this practice of giving as part of your child's early environment, they will accept the fact that giving is as natural as breathing and is simply part of how their family operates.

Developmental Tips
Ages 3–7

♦ Giving begins at home. It is very important that a child be allowed and expected to give. Let your young child give to you and the family.

♦ An important lesson to teach at this age is for them to give their *attention* when others are speaking.

- Children this age are concrete thinkers. Teach them to share things like cars, actions figures, dolls, or books as an act of service.

- They love to explore and touch their environment.

- They learn best by observation and repetition.

- Children this age learn a great deal through play-acting and storytelling.

- They learn by imitation. Demonstrate what you want them to learn, then let them try.

- Hands-on, tangible projects are best.

- Children this age need to see the recipients of their giving.

- Praise them for their accomplishments.

- Encourage small acts of giving daily—make it a habit.

- Make it fun.

Chapter Eight

Time to Share

Simple Ways for Children Ages 3-7 to Give Their Time

- Sorting for recycling.

- Cleaning up trash around home or school.

- Taking care of pets at home.

- Offering snacks and drinks to project workers where Mom and Dad volunteer.

- Making birthday cards for family and friends.

- Helping with simple household chores (dusting with feather duster, picking up clothes around the house, putting away plastic cups from the dishwasher).

- Making a coupon for an act of giving using their crayons and paper (silverware on table, picking up toys, hug).

- Visiting a neighbor and sharing a song or homemade cookies during Christmastime.

- Filling bird feeders.

- Helping pack up food items at Thanksgiving for a family in need.

- Collecting books for their age group and giving to a local school or shelter.

- Participating with the family in larger projects (Bear Hugs Project—teddies for police cars).

- Visiting an apple farm and collecting apples to give to family and friends for Rosh Hashanah.

- Helping weed the garden.

- Bringing a plant to brighten the day for an older person.

- Starting a neighborhood "Share the food" program by designating an item a month (i.e., tuna fish) to be dropped at a neighbor's and then taken to a local food bank. Let your younger child help collect, sort, and drop off. This is a great way to meet the neighbors as well!

♦ Picking up trash at a park—make it a counting game!

Chapter Nine

Talented Tots

Simple Ways for Children Ages 3-7 to Share Their Talent

+ Drawing a picture for a loved one.

+ Delivering a drawing, flower, or small token to a beloved relative, Sunday School teacher, or preschool teacher.

+ Decorating lunch bags for siblings' lunches.

+ Making bookmarks for friends and relatives as a Hanukkah project.

+ Putting together a "hospital cheer" bag for a child their own age.

+ Singing a song for friends.

+ Coloring a picture for family members for Christmas.

+ Dressing up and putting on a short play for an older neighbor.

+ Making someone in the family a simple snack.

Chapter Ten

Treasure Hunting and Helping

Simple Ways for Ages 3-7 to Share Their Treasure

At this age, the treasure children have is what you give them. They don't understand money as an exchange until they are about five or six years old.

- Let them help you with a garage sale and keep what they earn. Let them decide where to give away a portion.

- Set up three clear glass giving jars labeled: today, tomorrow, and giving. This will teach children simple ways to manage their treasure. Today's jar is money allocated for today's spending, tomorrow's jar is for the beginning of savings for the future, and the giving jar is to teach right from the beginning that part of what we have is to give away. The clear glass also allows the child to see the money as it accumulates.

- Encourage them to share a favorite toy with a sister or brother.

- Try Moonjar (http://www.moonjar.com) to order their special money box. The story behind Moonjar starts with John D. Rockefeller, who kept three jars for his children's allowances—one for saving, one for spending, and one for charitable giving. This model of managing money, paired with the legacy of her family's financial management principles, moved Mrs. Scandiuzzi to create Moonjar.

- Give them money to put in the offering plate at your place of worship.

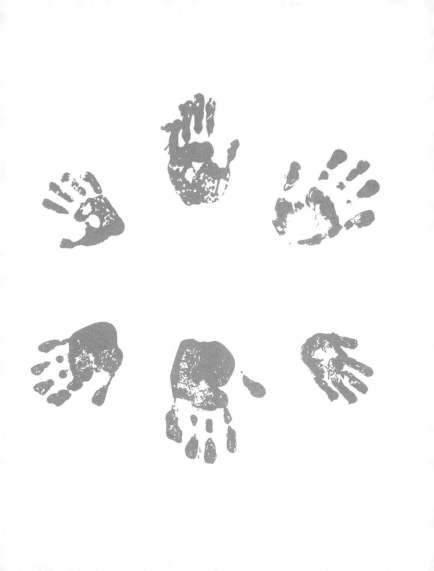

Chapter Eleven

Resources

Ages 3-7

Picture Books:

♦ Barker, Marjorie. *Magical Hands*. New York: Picture Book Studio Ltd., 1989.

William the Cooper has a special way of celebrating the birthdays of his friends. Read and find out what happens on his birthday.

♦ Brown, Marcia. *Stone Soup*. New York: Simon and Schuster, 1947.

Three hungry soldiers outwit a greedy village and teach a lesson about sharing.

♦ Lionni, Leo. *Swimmy*. New York: Alfred A. Knopf, 1963. Swimmy organizes the school of fish so they can protect themselves. This story is told in the usual delightful Lionni style.

♦ Porter, Barbara. *Miss Rumphius*. New York: Puffin Books, 1982.

A young girl named Alice grows into a wise old woman who searches for a way to make the world a more beautiful place.

♦ Pfister, Marcus. *The Rainbow Fish*. New York: North-South Books, 1992.

A beautiful multicolored fish learns to make friends by sharing.

Movies:

♦ *The Fox and the Hound*. Dir. Ted Berman. Perf. Mickey Rooney, Kurt Russell, and Pearl Bailey. Disney Studios, 1981.

Tod, a young fox, is raised by a kindly old lady after being orphaned. He meets a hound puppy and they become friends. As they grow up, problems begin to arise.

◆ *The Land Before Time*. Dir. Don Bluth. Perf. Candace Hutson, Judith Barsi, and Gabriel Damon. Lucas/Spielberg, 1988.

Littlefoot sets off in search of the Great Valley, encountering four other small dinosaurs that go on the adventure with him. Along the way they learn valuable lessons about sharing and working together.

◆ *Charlotte's Web*. Dir. Charles A. Nichols. Perf. Debbie Reynolds, Paul Lynde, and Henry Gibson. Paramount Studios, 1973.

Charlotte the Spider helps Wilbur the Pig escape his fate as pork chops for breakfast. This is a classic story of friendship and giving.

- *The Never Ending Story.* Dir. Wolfgang Petersen. Perf. Barret Oliver, Noah Hathaway, and Thomas Hill. Warner Bros, 1984.

  Bastian escapes his dreary world through an encounter with a magic book. In the land of Fantasia, he becomes a hero and learns who he really is.

- *Beauty and the Beast.* Dir. Gary Trousdale. Perf. Paige O'Hara, Robbie Benson, and Richard White. Disney Studios, 1991.

  Belle is a young girl who is more interested in reading than marrying. Her father, an inventor, gets lost in the forest and is imprisoned by the Beast. Belle must rescue him and ends up meeting, loathing, and then loving the Beast. This is a beautiful retelling of the classic fairy tale.

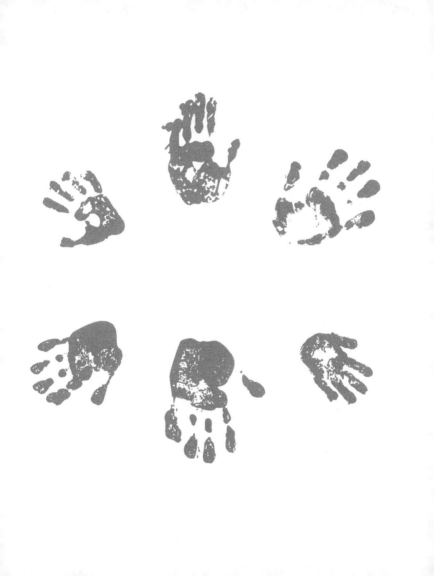

Chapter Twelve

Growing Givers

Ages 8-12

"How wonderful it is that nobody needs to wait a single moment before starting to improve the world."

—*Anne Frank*

*M*om, will you teach me to crochet? What are we go-ing to do now? I've decided to be a dancer. Stephanie is taking lessons, can I go, too? Dad, I need to make a race car for school, will you help me? Can I take karate? The poet Wordsworth made the observation that each child came "trail-ing clouds of glory." We could easily paraphrase that obser-vation to read, each elementary school child comes "trailing whirlwinds of energy."

This is the season of life when you live in your car, feeling like an unappreciated taxi service. You also spend so much time waiting for lessons, practices, and appointments that you could needle-point a life-sized tapestry of the state of Texas.

What's a parent to do? Enjoy it! It means your child is develop-mentally on track. If a child has had early needs met, he or she will arrive at this stage of development eagerly pursuing knowl-edge and full of initiative.

The growing giver has an innate desire to expand his or her horizons, learn new skills, and make new friends. It is an age of enterprise and industry. It is also the perfect age for children to move toward the outside world by offering their contributions to a world that desperately needs what young people have to give: youth, enthusiasm, energy, and joy.

Your children still look to you as their primary role model at this stage. Very shortly, they will look to their peers for affirmation, but up until about age twelve, their moms and dads are their chief examples of how to live.

Right now is the prime time to show your children what generosity looks like by getting them involved in volunteering with you as their partner. Getting involved with volunteering will help you in your quest to grow good kids who are good givers, too.

Developmental Tips

Ages 8–12

- ♦ They have lots of energy.

- ♦ They are expanding in their capacity to understand the world and are developing problem-solving skills.

- ♦ They are beginning to be able to reason and are becoming increasingly able to set goals.

- ♦ They are becoming more responsible and want to develop their personal interests and abilities.

- ♦ Their social network is expanding, and it needs your support.

- ♦ They are beginning to connect with the outside world and need to be encouraged to join youth groups and sports teams.

- ♦ They begin to relate to other adults besides Mom and Dad, and this enriches their world.

- Sharing friendships and working in a group are important to this age group when planning a service project.

- Children begin to develop empathy at this stage.

- Children this age like discussing the work of giving as well as doing it.

- They like to try new things.

- They are beginning to develop a sense of identity and want to be involved in choosing what they give to.

- This is the time for them to learn to give to the family through at least one daily responsibility (or "chore").

Chapter Thirteen

Time to Care

Simple Ways for Ages 8-12 to Give Their Time

- Join a wildlife organization together.

- Help them take care of a neighbor's pet.

- Help them find out about birds in the neighborhood— learn to recognize the common species and what they eat and need. Set out food and water.

- Join a recycling contest together: Great Paper Chase, Bottle Up, or Great Balls of Foil.

- Have them load and unload the dishwasher.

- Suggest they put together a simple puzzle with a younger child.

- Help them sort and pack food at a food bank.

- Encourage them to sort for recycling at school or home.

- Help them conduct an Easter egg hunt for the neighborhood kids.

- Volunteer with your child at the local animal shelter.

- Help them collect holiday items within your faith tradition to be distributed to those in need.

- Suggest they create a birthday surprise package for a child who would not otherwise have a celebration (for a child at a shelter, lower-income school, or hospital).

- Encourage them to carry groceries for seniors.

- Help them remove graffiti from walls or buildings.

- Find opportunities, with your encouragement, for them to listen, listen, listen as a way to give (to friends, neighbors, seniors, siblings, younger kids).

- Have them play card games with seniors or family.

- Suggest they hand out water or make granola bags for runners participating in their favorite charity runs.

Chapter Fourteen

Talented Preteens

Simple Ways for Ages 8-12 to Share Their Talent

- Help the artistic ones design and paint a mural for their school.

- Help them start a buddy program at their school.

- Have them make and decorate a holiday cake for someone special.

- Encourage them to play their instruments at a senior care center.

- Suggest tutoring younger children in a subject they are good in.

- Suggest being a teacher's helper: for a semester, have them visit their favorite teacher one time per week to do odd jobs around the classroom.

- Help them design and make a "new kid" survival kit for kids new to their school.

- Encourage them to teach their favorite sport to a young elementary school child.

- Have them create greeting cards for family and friends.

- Suggest they build a dreidel for a younger sibling during Hanukkah.

- Help them establish a "secret friend" day.

- Encourage them to decorate flower pots for assisted living centers.

- Suggest they make flashcards for students/adults in English as a Second Language classes.

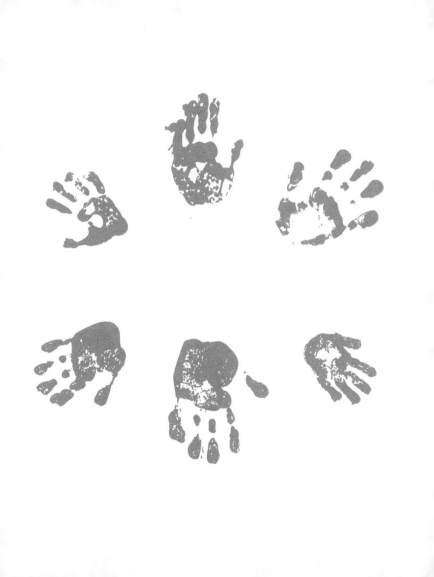

Chapter Fifteen

Treasure to Measure

Simple Ways for Ages 8-12
to Share Their Treasure

Treasure

♦ Encourage them to help with a recycling effort and donate the money they receive to their school.

♦ Suggest that they plant a tree in honor of someone.

♦ Help them raise money to purchase books for the library of an underprivileged school.

♦ Help your child set up a lemonade stand and give the profits to the local YMCA.

♦ Encourage them to share some of their lunch money with a friend in need.

♦ Suggest that they donate part of their birthday or holiday money to a nonprofit they love—help them decide which one.

- Encourage them to use some of their money to buy holiday presents for family and friends.

- Giving an allowance each week helps your child start to set goals for managing and giving their money. If you choose to give an allowance for the work they do around the home, still have them do something to give to the family that is not part of their allowance. This allows them to practice the habit of giving.

Chapter Sixteen

Resources

Ages 8-12

Books:

♦ Ash, Russell. *Aesop's Fables*. Chronicle Books, 1990.
A child-friendly edition of the collection of famous parables by the Greek slave. Every child deserves to think about and discuss the "Lion and the Mouse," the "Tortoise and the Hare," and the "Sun and the Wind" with his or her parents.

♦ Burnett, F. H. *The Secret Garden*. New York: Harper-Collins Children's Books, 1911.
Orphaned in India, Mary Lennox goes to live with Colin, an invalid. She discovers a secret garden and slowly brings it back to life with the help of the gardener's son, Dickon. As the garden recovers, so does the fretful Colin. A tender story about giving and compassion.

♦ L'Engle, Madeleine. *A Wrinkle in Time*. New York: Farrar, Straus, Giroux, 1961.

A classic story of giving set in a science fiction space/time adventure. Twelve-year-old Meg learns how to give and saves the life of her beloved youngest brother, Charles Wallace.

♦ Lewis, C. S. *The Chronicles of Narnia*. New York: HarperCollins Children's Books, 1955.

A classic series of seven stories about the magical adventures of the Pevensie children in the land of Narnia. These books provide wonderful insights into character development, courage, and generosity. Don't miss sharing them with your child.

- Lowry, Lois. *The Giver*. New York: Houghton Mifflin Co., 1993.

  A young boy is chosen to receive the memories of his people. They prove disturbing to him as he begins to remember a time when their collective life was not so perfect or controlled.

- McDonald, George. *The Light Princess*. Canada: Douglas & McIntyre Ltd., 1864.

  A princess, born to a king and queen, is cursed at birth with a lack of gravity. She is saved from her "light" world by a prince who loves her enough to help her find her gravity. A delightful story that leaves the reader with much to think about.

Movies:

♦ *The Lion, the Witch and the Wardrobe.* Dir. Andrew Adamson. Perf. Georgie Henley, William Moseley, and Tilda Swinton. Buena Vista Home Entertainment, 2005.

Book One of the Chronicles of Narnia. The Pevensie children are sent away to the professor's house in the country during World War II in Britain. They explore an old wardrobe and fall into the country of Narnia. This movie has themes of courage, resourcefulness, and redemption.

♦ *The Rookie.* Dir. John Lee Hancock. Perf. Dennis Quaid, Rachel Griffiths, and Jay Hernandez. Walt Disney Video, 2002.

Based on the true story of Jim Morris, a Texas high school baseball coach who makes a deal with his second-rate team. If they go to the state championship, Jim will try out for professional baseball. The team wins, and Morris gets another chance at his dream.

- *The Lord of the Rings*. Dir. Peter Jackson. Perf. Elijah Wood, Sean Astin, and Ian McKellan. New Line Cinema, 2005.
  This trilogy is a grand adventure with themes of loyalty, courage, wisdom, and generosity.

- *Pay It Forward*. Dir. Mimi Leder. Perf. Kevin Spacey, Helen Hunt, Haley Joel Osment. Warner Home Video, 2001.
  A young boy in difficult circumstances takes up a challenge from his teacher to think of a way to change the world. He does three acts of kindness to three different people and then asks them to "pay it forward" to three other people. Illustrates the power of generosity.

- *E.T. the Extra Terrestrial.* Dir. Steven Spielberg. Perf. Henry Thomas, Dee Wallace, and Drew Barrymore. Universal Studios, 1982.

  A little alien is left behind on Earth when his spaceship departs. He is befriended by Elliott, a young boy who lives with his siblings and single mother in a very ordinary suburban subdivision. As E.T. and Elliott grow to be friends, a special task force is scouring the country looking for this alien life-form. E.T. longs for home, and the children help him find a way back. Themes of friendship, sacrifice, and loyalty.

- *Old Yeller.* Dir. Robert Stevenson. Perf. Dorothy McGuire, Fess Parker, and Tommy Kirk. Walt Disney Video, 1957.

  Travis Coates befriends a yellow mongrel dog that wanders onto their Texas ranch in the 1860s. Themes of loyalty and faithfulness.

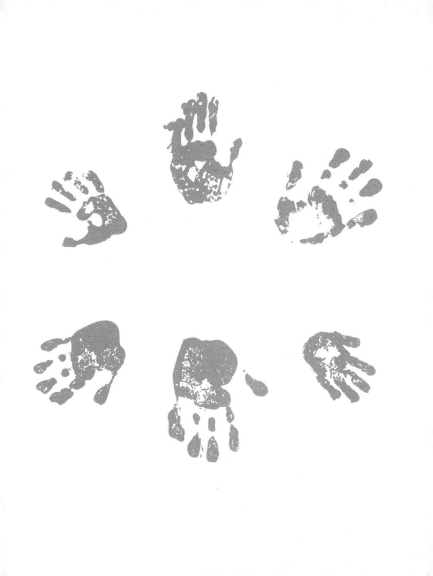

Chapter Seventeen

Middle School Madness

Ages 13-15

"You must give some time to your fellow men. Even if it's a little thing, do something for others—something for which you get no pay but the privilege of doing it."

—*Albert Schweitzer*

P ity the dad who comes down to breakfast one morning and discovers that his son or daughter has been abducted by aliens, leaving a surly, monosyllabic creature in his or her place. While his child once cheerfully communicated about school, friends, and activities, this strange creature speaks only in one-syllable grunts:

"How was school today?"

"Fine."

"How was the dance?"

"OK."

"Did you do well on the test?"

"Yep."

Welcome to the middle school years, when your child is held captive by hormonal surges and cares only about what "everybody else" (except you) thinks and does. Take comfort in the fact that your child will eventually emerge from these years and most likely become a charming, fully-functional, articulate adult. Meanwhile, there is enjoyment to be had in his or her enthusiasm, sense of humor, and sheer exuberance.

Early adolescence is a time of testing and experimentation. Young teenagers are experiencing the roller coaster ride of hormones, growth spurts, and fitting in. One day all is well, the next day it is the end of their world. The only distinguishing factor might be that their current crush sat with someone else at lunch. Sometimes their mood shifts from high to low in an hour, sometimes less.

When your child is so intensely focused on "me, me, me," how do you get her to look up from her navel and notice the outside world? What is true in training horses also seems to be true with adolescents: a sideways move is best. Walking in on a Saturday morning with the announcement, "We're gonna be more compassionate around here, and we're starting by volunteering at the shelter every Sunday afternoon," won't work.

It is appropriate to expect your middle school child to volunteer, but at this age, they need a say in where they invest their time. A place to start is to observe their interests. Do they like sports, animals, or fashion? Starting with their interests, brainstorm ways they could be involved in volunteer efforts in those areas. You could say something like, "We're going to volunteer somewhere together, any ideas where you would like to give?"

Middle school-aged kids need hands-on experiences to hold their interest and help them learn. Their abstract reasoning skills are only partially developed. In terms of volunteering, that means that they have to have an emotional connection with their project. Most importantly, they need to see how their volunteering has helped to make a difference.

Social interaction is important to the middle school student. Volunteering with a group is often a successful approach. Doing something worthwhile for someone else while in the company of their friends helps offset the boredom factor and their short attention spans. If you take this into account, you have a chance to imprint the habit of giving on your child through an enjoyable experience. This can set the stage for being involved in volunteering in high school and beyond.

Developmental Tips
Ages 13–15

- This is an age of experimentation; they need to be given the opportunity to try different kinds of giving situations.

- They like to work in groups.

- They want to be socially engaged and make a difference.

- Don't expect them to stick with one project for an extended period—they have short attention spans.

- They want to decide where to volunteer based on their interests and what their friends are doing—this is good.

- Preplanning is crucial for an event to be successful with this age group.

- Stuffing envelopes will not work—young adolescents need to be connected to real world activities (and people) for giving to feel meaningful.

- They need an adult advocate who will lobby for their need to do important volunteer work that is within their skill and responsibility level.

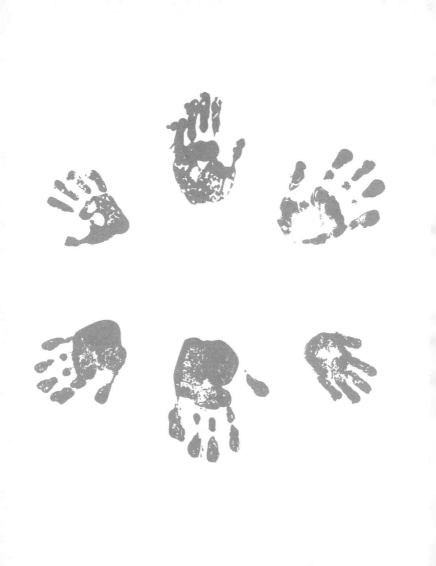

Chapter Eighteen

Time to Spare

Simple Ways for Ages 13-15 to Give Their Time

Encourage them to:

♦ Volunteer through Scouts.

♦ Work with local shelters and collect items for "basics bags"—kits for needy people.

♦ Be a single parent helper and find out where they can contribute to another family (through babysitting, mowing the lawn, or helping with homework).

♦ Make first-day-of-school bags for low-income students or students at their school.

♦ Use the principle that laughter is the best medicine and create a "Laugh Pack" for a sick child or senior.

♦ Be a buddy to a younger student.

♦ Adopt a family and be their "secret Santa" at Christmas.

- Play bingo or pool with a senior.

- Babysit for free for a family that could use their "gift" of time.

- Help a busy mom clean out her garage (or, how about their own mom or dad?).

- Watch a movie with a younger sibling.

- Help at a local food bank stocking shelves.

- Do yard work around the house without being asked.

- Make lunches for a homeless shelter once a month.

- Rake leaves for a neighbor.

- Volunteer at a local thrift store (often benefiting hospitals, schools, shelters, etc.).

- Clean up around a place of worship.

♦ Trick or treat for UNICEF.

♦ Adopt an angel from the Salvation Army tree at Christmas.

♦ Get involved at a community event and volunteer with the whole family.

Chapter Nineteen

Talented Teens

Simple Ways for Ages 13-15 to Share Their Talent

Encourage them to:

- Tutor younger students at a subject they excel in.

- Make a poison control tip list for the kitchen.

- Bake their best batch of cookies, under your supervision, for a teacher.

- Put together a car safety kit for the family.

- Create holiday craft kits for disadvantaged or hospitalized kids.

- Make a birthday present for a friend.

- Make ornaments for senior citizens or teachers.

- Start a "Safety First" babysitting club.

- Decorate a friend's locker for his birthday.

- ♦ Make valentine card surprises for friends or relatives.

- ♦ Make fleece blankets for kids in a children's hospital.

- ♦ Paint pumpkins for neighbors at Halloween.

- ♦ Bake matzo and use it in special food baskets for Passover to give to assisted living centers and to people who can't afford food.

- ♦ Organize a blanket drive for a local shelter.

- ♦ Sew a pillow or make a craft for a grandparent or great-grandparent.

- ♦ Play for a senior center (if they have musical talent).

- ♦ Draw or paint a picture for a family member or friend (if they have artistic talent).

- ♦ Take a younger student to the library and help them check out books.

- Read to younger children or seniors—and make it interesting.

- Coach younger kids in a sport they excel in.

- Make and bring dinner to a neighbor.

- Show an older person how to use their computer, cell phone, or iPod.

Chapter Twenty

Treasure to Save and Give

Simple Ways for Ages 13-15
to Share their Treasure

Encourage them to:

♦ Start a Parent/Child Philanthropy Club (be sure to explain this word to your kids); consider joining together with other families to make larger donations and to make the giving more fun.

♦ Do a gift-wrapping fundraiser for a special cause.

♦ Give a gift in honor of a favorite teacher or relative to a charity of choice.

♦ Organize a walk-a-thon or bike-a-thon for a cause they believe in.

♦ Organize a "dress-down" day, where students pay for this privilege and donate the proceeds to a charity of their choice.

- Buy a flower for a friend who had a bad day.

- Buy a trinket for their sister "just because."

- Research twelve different causes they believe in and donate to a different charity once a month for a year.

- Hold a car wash, either with a club they belong to or with friends, and then decide together where to donate the money.

- Have a yard sale and use the money to give back.

- Hold a kids' art auction with artwork created by them and their friends; allow for silent bidding with an easy display of the art and have the money raised go to the local SPCA.

♦ Set up a marathon event of some kind (watermelon-eating contest, hula hoop, spelling bee, etc.) with people pledging to raise money.

♦ Sell flowers for Valentine's Day and donate the money to a heart-related charity, maybe a local pediatric cardiac care unit.

♦ Try designating a certain percentage of all the money they earn or receive to a cause they believe in (or pick several).

♦ Set up a haunted house and use the entry fee to buy goods to stock a food pantry.

♦ Raise money to buy and plant trees to help celebrate Arbor Day.

Chapter Twenty-One

Resources

Ages 13-15

Books:

♦ Andersen, Hans Christian. *The Little Mermaid and other Fairy Tales*. Viking. 1998.

A collection of Andersen's fairy tales: timeless in their themes of sacrifice, generosity, and love.

♦ Sachar, Louis. *Holes*. New York: Random House Children's Books, 1998.
Stanley Yelnats is sent to Camp Green Lake for stealing a pair of sneakers he didn't steal. The Yelnats always have bad luck. This is a funny, gritty, surprising story of redemption that takes some unusual twists and turns.

♦ Saint-Exupéry, Antoine de. *The Little Prince*. New York: Harcourt Inc., 1943.
A classic fable about the meaning of loving and caring for others, delightfully illustrated by the author.

+ Speare, Elizabeth George. *The Bronze Bow*. New York: Houghton Mifflin, 1961.

   A story set in long-ago Palestine, Daniel is a young boy who hates his Roman oppressors. He joins a band of revolutionaries and in the process comes to terms with suffering and learns what true freedom means.

Movies:

+ *Holes*. Dir. Andrew Davis. Perf. Sigourney Weaver, Jon Voight, Shia LeBeouf. Disney Home DVD, 2003.

   Nerdy Stanley Yelnats is sent to Camp Green Lake for stealing a pair of sneakers. An unlikely, gritty and entertaining story of redemption set in a bleak West Texas detention camp for delinquents.

- *I Am David*. Dir. Paul Feig. Perf. Ben Tibber, James Cav-
  iezel, and Joan Plowright. Lions Gate, 2005.

  This is the story of a twelve-year-old boy who escapes
  from a communist concentration camp and travels across
  Europe, living by his wits. Full of fear at first, he gradually
  learns to trust the people he encounters and let them
  help him.

- *My Dog Skip*. Dir. Jay Russell. Perf. Frankie Muniz,
  Diane Lane, Kevin Bacon, and Luke Wilson. Warner
  Bros. Studio, 2002.

  Willie Morris has a hard luck life in Yazoo, Mississippi,
  until he "adopts" Skip. Together, Willie and Skip conquer
  their world.

Chapter Twenty-Two

Making It Cool to Give in High School

Giving for Ages 16–18

"An attitude of gratitude creates blessings. Help yourself by helping others. You have the most powerful weapons on earth, love and prayer."

—*John Templeton*

As your child matures through the teen years, the brain continues to develop and there are fleeting moments of adult-like thinking. Notice we said "fleeting."

In the midst of the excitement of sports, proms, and learning to drive, important questions are being raised and answered: "What am I good at?" "What do I have to give?" "What do I want to give?" "Who is that cute new boy?" "Am I a giving person?" "What shall I wear to school tomorrow?" "Who is going to invite me to the prom?"

If you think of a stained glass window, with its varied colors and shapes, which, when viewed from a distance, make a pleasing whole, you will have an idea of how their identities are coming together.

This is not to say that you won't get cut on some of the sharper edges, and you may not like the color combinations, but this is all part of the healthy personality development of the later teenage years

Students are experimenting with what they like to give, all in the context of self-discovery and identity formation. In this apprenticeship to adulthood, parents are still very important, but their involvement may take the form of being emotionally supportive rather than lending their physical presence to volunteer activities.

Remember, developing the habit of giving is critical to their well-being as adults—and you can still help them!

Developmental Tips
Ages 16–18

- This is the age for direct experience.

- Supervision is still necessary, but older teenagers can take on many parts of planning a giving opportunity.

- Talk with your teenager about what charities move their heart.

- Encourage them to get involved in the planning council of their youth group so they can have a say in volunteer projects.

- Talk with your teenager about the difference community service makes in your town.

- Support their efforts to be independent and find their own way of giving.

- Encourage them to "take on" a project that seems bigger than they are.

- Be there to provide GUIDANCE—not to do it for them.

- Expect them to make mistakes and get off-track. It is an important learning experience.

- Use topics of interest to them to jump-start discussions about giving with your older teen.

Chapter Twenty-Three

Time to Dare

Ideas for Giving Time for Ages 16-18

Encourage them to:

♦ Be a hospital companion.

♦ Visit a nursing home on a regular basis.

♦ Assist animal keepers at the zoo.

♦ Mentor a younger student.

♦ Read to children at a local hospital.

♦ Volunteer time at a homeless shelter.

♦ Organize a drive to collect donations.

♦ Serve dinner at a local shelter on a day *other* than Thanksgiving or Christmas.

♦ Work with animal rescue centers.

♦ Help at Special Olympics events.

- Deliver menorahs and candles to the senior centers.

- Telephone for a telethon of their choice.

- Help an elderly neighbor:

  - Mow the lawn, pull weeds, or do jobs around their house.

  - Grocery shop, pick up prescriptions, or help to take care of pets.

  - Shovel snow, write letters and checks, or just listen to what they have to say.

- Paint over graffiti.

- Adopt a section of park or highway and maintain it.

- Monitor pH levels in nearby water.

- Make emergency kits for home or school.

- Volunteer to rock and cuddle babies at low-income child care centers.

- Make new mother kits for single mothers at the local hospital.

- Encourage a friend who is trying to lose weight.

- Write a note to a friend who needs cheering up or to a sibling at college.

- Make gift baskets for seniors.

Chapter Twenty-Four

Talented Teens Part Two

Possibilities for Talented Giving for Ages 16–18

Encourage them to:

♦ Play poker with seniors.

♦ Assist in an after-school league for younger children in a sport they like.

♦ Organize a Walk-a-thon for a favorite charity.

♦ Volunteer to help teach computer literacy to younger students.

♦ With their friends or youth group, adopt and repair a worn-out playground in a poor part of their city.

♦ Recycle bicycles.

♦ Play guitar at a faith service.

♦ Bake potato latkes (pancakes) for family for Hanukkah.

♦ Help an older person record memories.

♦ Sew pajamas for a younger sibling.

♦ Help bake cookies or brownies for blood drive volunteers.

- Organize a grandparents' day for a local elementary school (or their own).

- Conduct nature walks at the local botanical garden.

- Tutor younger students in an area they excel in.

- Teach first aid or water safety.

- For those fluent in a second language, suggest volunteering to translate at hospitals or government centers.

- Learn sign language to work with the deaf.

- Perform a dance recital for seniors or an after-school program.

- Knit or crochet scarves or blankets for seniors.

- Put together a band to play at a charity or holiday event.

- Start an "E-cycling event" for recycling electronics.

- Create a play and perform it as a benefit for a favorite charity.

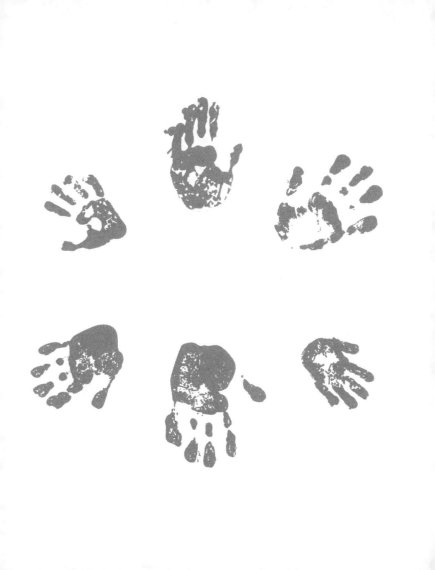

Chapter Twenty-Five

Treasure to Multiply

Giving Opportunities for Ages 16–18

- Consider matching any amount your teen donates to a charity or non-profit organization.

- Teach them what your family tradition is concerning giving and let them know how you give, and to what causes.

- Encourage them to sell great lunches, pizza, or ice cream to raise money for favorite charities.

- Suggest they sell candy grams as a fundraiser for a good cause.

- Have them consider donating proceeds from karaoke night to fund a favorite charity.

- Encourage them to have a student art sale to raise money for a worthy cause.

♦ Suggest they check out the "Empty Bowls" fundraiser for a unique approach to raising money for charity—http://www.emptybowls.com.

♦ Have them consider different collections for worthy causes and to make up their own names (i.e., Infant Needs—Baby Shower in a Box):

1. Housewares drive (sheets, towels, pillows, dishes, etc.) for a refugee apartment or for someone coming out of a shelter.

2. Collect art supplies (paints, watercolors, markers, crayons, clay, paper) for a needy local school or daycare center.

3. Health care drive (band aids, alcohol wipes, shampoo, conditioners, soaps, toothpaste) for homeless shelters and low income medical clinics.

4. Infant needs (diapers, formula, crib sheets, blankets, clothes, toys, shampoo, bottles, bibs, pacifiers) for women's shelters and pregnancy centers.

- Start a "make a change" drive for something important to your student and his or her school by having everyone donate spare change to a worthy cause.

Chapter Twenty-Six

Resources

Ages 16-18

Books:

♦ Beckett, Sister Wendy. *Sister Wendy's Book of Saints*. Dorling Kindersley, 1998.
Sister Wendy talks about thirty-five saints with illustrations and text describing their stories of courage and bravery.

♦ Bolden, Tonya. *And Not Afraid to Dare: The Stories of Ten African American Women*. Scholastic, 1998.
These are the remarkable stories of ten African-American women who overcame adversity through persistence and courage.

♦ Lee, Harper. *To Kill a Mockingbird*. New York: Harper Collins, 1960.
A white, Southern family suffers when their father, a prominent attorney, defends a black man unjustly accused of rape. This is a classic that will have you crying one minute and laughing the next.

- Lewis, Clive Staples. *The Space Trilogy*. New York: Scribner's Book Co., 1938.

   This is a classic space trilogy that is fascinating science fiction fantasy as well as a cleverly told philosophical treatise on the nature of good and evil.

- Sullivan, Dan. *The Gratitude Principle*. The Strategic Coach, 2006.

   This is a book that discusses the role of gratitude in building a lifetime of appreciation. It comes with a CD for easy drive-time listening.

Movies:

- *Gandhi*. Dir. Richard Attenborough. Perf. Ben Kingsley, Candice Bergen, and Edward Fox. Sony Pictures, 1982.

   This is a compelling film about a humble lawyer who made a huge impact on the world by embracing nonviolence as a way to affect political change. Inspiring.

- *Babette's Feast*. Dir. Gabriel Alex. Perf. Stephane Audran, Birgitte Federspiel. MGM, 1999.
In this classic story about generosity, an expatriate Frenchwoman is taken in and befriended by two sisters in a remote Scandinavian fishing village. Their kindness is amply repaid when their servant decides to surprise them with a sumptuous meal worthy of the finest Parisian restaurants.

- *The Man from Snowy River*. Dir. George Miller. Perf. Tom Burlinson, Terence Donovan, and Kirk Douglas. Twentieth Century Fox, 1982.
The story of a young man from the mountains of Australia who has to prove himself through hardship when his father dies. An old-fashioned coming-of-age story complete with a satisfying love story. Great fun.

- *To Kill a Mockingbird*. Dir. Robert Mulligan. Perf. Gregory Peck, John Megna, and Frank Overton. Universal Pictures, 1962.

  One of the finest American films ever made. This movie presents an emotionally riveting portrayal of the power of justice, integrity, and love in the face of injustice and evil. Watch it together.

- *Schindler's List*. Dir. Steven Spielberg. Perf. Liam Neeson, Ben Kingsley, and Ralph Fiennes. Universal Studios, 1993.

  The horrifying yet uplifting story of Oskar Schindler, a member of the Nazi party, who saved 1,100 Jews from the concentration camps by employing them in his wartime pottery factory. A meditation on how one man can make a difference.

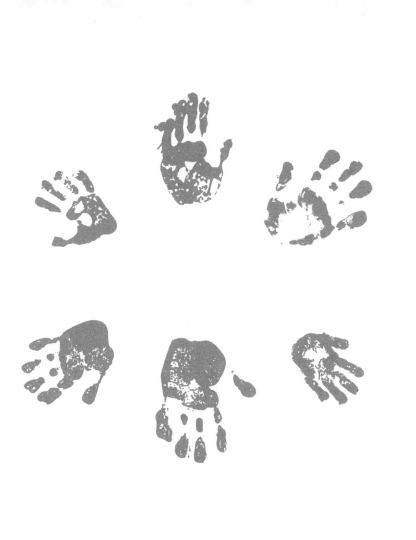

Section Three

Giving in Action

Inspiring stories, quotes from all ages,
more practical tips, and giving resources.

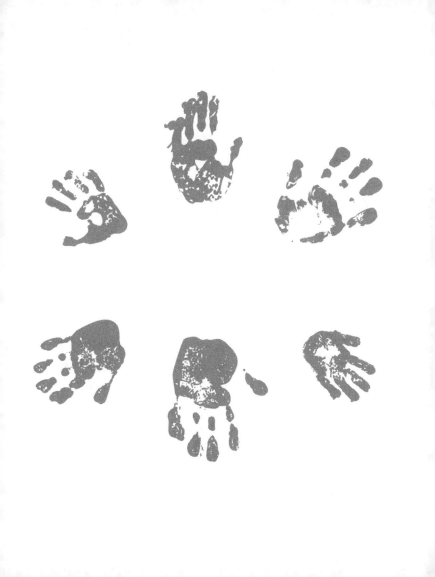

Chapter Twenty-Seven

Making a Huge Difference

M eet Ryan, who decided it would be good to give rather than accumulate gifts. With his bar mitzvah approaching, Ryan and his mom talked about the option of using this special time to focus on giving to others.

He helped organize a group of approximately twenty-five friends and family members who agreed that, rather than exchanging gifts among themselves for their bar and bat mitzvahs, each of their families would make contributions to a Donor Advised Charitable Fund, from which the kids would make grants to deserving non-profit organizations.

Following a previously used model and with the help of two parents, the students organized their own group and worked through the K-HELP Fund (Kids Helping Everyone Live Peacefully). They held regular meetings and learned so much more than just how to write a check!

Here are just a few of the things they learned:

- How to run a meeting (Roberts Rules of Order).

- How to recognize different types of organizations (profit, non-profit, governmental).

- How to determine which charities they would give to.

- How to collaborate and let others share their opinion (a form of giving in itself).

- How to help fund worthwhile causes (and maybe contribute in other ways as well).

- How to share their views passionately and make decisions.

- How it feels to see generosity in action.

The response was FANTASTIC! In all, the fund received donations of more than $50,000. The kids decided to use the money to help children, provide hunger relief, and improve education. Organizations such as Ronald McDonald House, Kids to Kids (an Israeli group providing therapeutic services to children who are victims of terrorism), Gilda's Club of Dallas, and many more received grants.

Giving is contagious! Even more exciting was the inspiration this group of students had on those around them, both kids and adults! Another class has started its own fund and a group of families in another school has joined in. The model they used became the basis for a national presentation to hundreds of community foundation leaders.

As Ryan said, "I really enjoyed the fact that I could do this with my friends. It makes it much more fun to share with others. And, other than a few times when we needed help from the parents, we basically ran the show. That was good!

"I didn't realize how much influence twenty-five kids could have. A small amount of people and a small amount of money can make a huge difference. So even if something seems insignificant, give!"

Generous Kids Quotes

"I gave my friend a penny so we both had one."

Marvin—age 7

*"When I was 13, I was really sick and in the hospital.
I desperately needed a blood transfusion or might have not lived
through the night. My grandfather came all the way
to Houston to give me his blood, and because he did,
I am alive today."*

Charlie—age 19

*"To me giving means to share what you have, and also it has to
have love put into it."*

Justin—age 9

"Before the poetry contest, a teacher listened to me practice and gave me some really important tips and advice. It was because of this advice that I ended up winning in the District Meet."

Karla—age 16

"I gave my princess box to my friend Isabel, even though it was my favorite . . . and that day she was happy."

Julie—age 5

"I sent candy grams to a few underclassmen that were considered sort of dorky so that they could have a great Valentine's Day."

Amy—age 18

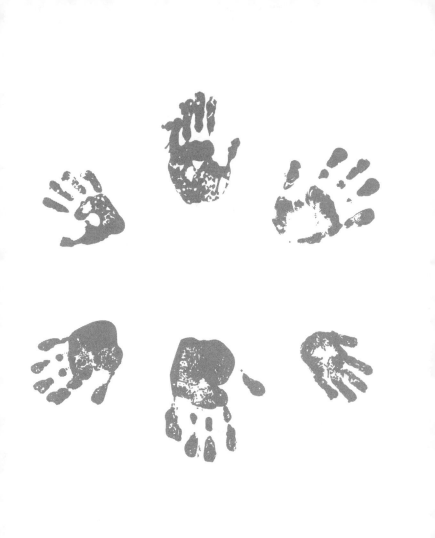

Chapter Twenty-Eight

Get that
Giving Feeling Going

H annah, a "*Generous Kid*" who leads by example, wants everyone to know that once you get the giving feeling going, you'll never want to stop!!!

When she was diagnosed with juvenile diabetes at the age of six, her parents decided to "make lemonade out of lemons." They immediately got involved in the Juvenile Diabetes Research Foundation, and Hannah led the way.

Hannah became the face of a disease that no child should have in his or her life. She has gone to company meetings where they were raising money for diabetes to talk about what she and her family have to go through every day: multiple blood tests, daily insulin injections, and middle-of-the-night blood checks. Hannah's presence makes the suffering caused by Juvenile Diabetes real to the audience. It touches their hearts, and generous giving is the result.

She and her family organize a team every year in conjunction with the national "Walk for the Cure" to raise awareness and money for juvenile diabetes. Why? "Because it helps everyone, not just me." And, as with most everything Hannah and her family do, they make it fun. Each year a new T-shirt is created: Hannah's Bananas, Hannah's Heroes, and Hannah's Hippies are just a few. Thousands of dollars are raised, and neighbors, families, and friends get to join together and give, spreading hope to many families.

Having diabetes helped Hannah learn the habit of giving early, and now what Hannah knows for sure is that giving is great, **especially** when you are passionate about the project! Here are some of Hannah's favorite examples:

- ♦ The Shoe Box Drive for orphans done through her church. Her passion for this charity? Because her brother is adopted, she knows there are good kids in orphanages that might miss Christmas. She and each of her family members fill shoe boxes with items for kids. Hannah especially likes filling hers with toys, books, pajamas, and coloring books. Many of those items are bought with her own money. "Praying over the box before it goes to the kids is a way of giving too."

♦ Reading Together™, a special literacy program where fifth graders help second graders improve their reading skills. Passion? This happens to be her brother's age, and she wants to be a teacher. Hannah says, "I get a good feeling inside doing something for someone else, and I get to help them see that this is going to be fun—to read!"

♦ "Hannah's Dance Class" is a special summer project. Why is she passionate about this? Because she loves to dance, and it was a way to give the parents of eight girls between the ages of six and nine a break. "It was really fun teaching them to dance. The only hard part was getting them under control! But they learned a lot, and I donated the money I made to Juvenile Diabetes Research. It's fun to find ways to give."

♦ Dog walking. Passion? "Is there anything better than when a dog licks your face? I love to do this, and it helps others out. Then I get to spend money on gifts for family and friends, and me."

♦ Writing songs/poems. Her passion? Sharing with others. Here's part of a poem that Hannah wrote when she was ten:

"A different kind of hero is someone with a soul.
With the strength of a mighty tiger,
And a heart that's made of gold.
So just look in yourself and there you'll see,
A hero living in you and me."

"It's also nice to do something nice for someone that no one else knows. My parents have taught me so much about giving to others. As my mom says, 'We're being a good neighbor.' That's all it takes."

Hannah would like parents to know "they should give their kids the gift of giving. If they don't know how to give, they are going to be selfish, and that's not any fun for the people around them."

Now twelve years old, Hannah, with a twinkle in her eyes and a smile on her face, will continue to be a youth ambassador for Juvenile Diabetes. She will continue speaking before the legislature, enjoying school youth council, finding new things to be passionate about, and discovering creative ways to give. "Adopt an attitude of gratitude. You'll feel better about yourself."

Generous Kids Quotes

"I was 14 years old and doing service in a nursing home and a man that I was visiting was telling me how nice it was to have someone to talk with. It made me feel good that I was helping him feel good."

Kitaro—age 16

"Boy Scout trip—I gave CPR—it saved a boy's life. I was in 8th grade and the boy was in 7th. He fell out of a canoe and went unconscious. When we got him out we called 911 and I revived him through CPR."

Scott—age 16

"I gave a cotton ball tower to my mom and my dad on their annivershuree [sic]. It made me feel good inside."

William—age 7

"Yesterday morning my mom was starting a new job and I wrote her a sign that said, 'Good morning Mom. I love you. You are a superhero mom. Thank you.' It was early and I was a little incoherent, but I think she liked it. I hope it made her day better."

Petra—age 16

"Giving means to me that if you give someone something you don't take it back."

Ernest—age 13

Chapter Twenty-Nine

Stepping Up

Addison asked the question that Generous Kids learn, "How can I help?" The question was asked to the principal of a small, low-income school. Her response as they were touring the school was: "We really could use new fire doors (a gasp came out of Addison's mouth) and new treads and risers on four flights of stairs. (The treads and risers are the rubber part that goes on the stair and the piece in front so students don't slip going up or coming down the stairs.) It's a big problem; the students catch their feet on the steps and could easily fall."

That's how this eighth grader started his Eagle Scout project. Not only would the actual work need to be done (which no one knew how to do), but money would need to be raised to help purchase the materials. Addison got busy.

It started with rallying the troops—literally! Addison spoke to his Boy Scout troop and told them about the situation at the little school. He asked for their assistance in raising money, getting tools and supplies, and actually doing the work.

While speaking to a local dad's club, Addison said, "I have no idea how to get this done; I just know it needs to be done, and I need help!" Well, he got help. His scout troop, family, friends, and the whole community pitched in to support.

Expertise was needed, and Addison found it in a flooring company that agreed to supply the materials at cost and send one of their people to help with the project once the work started.

Everyone pitched in. There were flyers to be made, church bulletins to be stuffed, and collection cans to be manned after church. Even after being told people would not be enthusiastic about "stairs," Addison and his fellow scouts kept going. They all learned a big lesson in persistence when an anonymous donor gave $1,000 because of their enthusiasm. In total, twenty scouts and friends helped to raise over $4,000 for the project!

When the weekend for the work came, parents, scouts, and friends showed up in droves to work. They started by taking off the old treads and risers. Then—breakdown. The expert from the flooring company was stranded out-of-town. The school could not be left in such disarray. Breakthrough—enter two dads in construction to step in and lend the guiding hands that were needed.

Over 300 hours went into the project. There were so many hands to help during the weekend that the additional volunteers were able to work on extra projects around the school. Walls and classrooms were scrubbed, yard work was taken care of, and the playground was cleaned up. Everyone helped. There was even money left over to purchase much-needed playground equipment.

Now in college, when asked about the project and the impact it had on him, Addison recalls, "What sticks out in my mind the most is the sense of community I found. There is something special to be said about the bond that is forged only through hard work. When people are working together for the benefit of others, they become stronger as a community. You find yourself connecting with others in a way that you would never find otherwise. This feeling reaches its pinnacle when that work is for others because one loses one's sense of self. As much as I personally took charge of this project, I know I was only one part of a whole."

Generous Kids Quotes

"I gave my brother love and support when he wanted to join the football team, and everyone else in the family told him it was too dangerous and he was too young. I gave my time when I went to every one of his games. My giving of love, time, and support to my brother made a difference in how much he believed in himself, his team won the championship, with him getting the winning touchdown."

Adrienne—age 15

"One time my friend didn't have lunch. I had my lunch but I didn't have any money left over. I decided to give him my lunch and I didn't eat."

George—age 14

"Last Christmas I bought earrings for my mother. I had to keep it a secret. That means not to say it to my mother. That's what my dad said to me on Christmas Eve."

Jamie—age 7

"When my mom was crying because of something that happened, I gave time to talk to her and see what happened. And by giving her a little present. It was a mood ring, so I can see when something was wrong."

Angie—age 12

"When I was about 8 I got a rock and my cousin was not allowed to get one for some reason, so I gave him mine."

Leslie—age 16

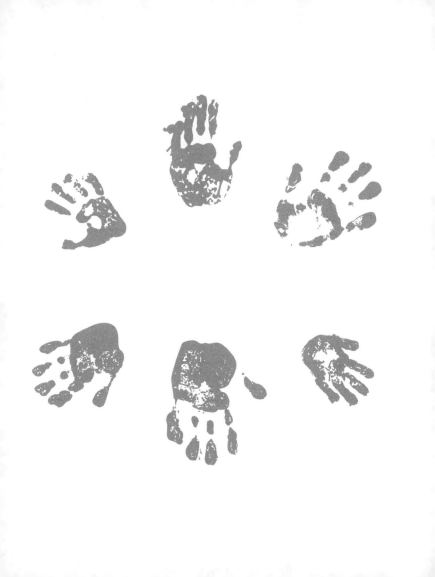

Chapter Thirty

Generations of Giving

Generous Kids

Maureen McClelland is a beautiful woman with bright blue eyes that sparkle when she is amused. Mrs. McClelland, widowed at a young age, raised her daughter Katie alone. What few people know about this dynamic duo is that they have logged hundreds of hours per year for many years volunteering.

Maureen made a conscious decision when Katie was young to make volunteering part of their family tradition, just as she had been raised to do. Volunteering and caring for others has been a part of the McClelland family for at least four generations. Her own parents were involved in giving and volunteering as far back as she can remember. Her family did not have much money, so volunteering their time was a way to give back to their community. Her family showed up at church spaghetti suppers, worked in the nursery, and volunteered in Little League events. Giving was a part of their life—it was fun.

Maureen has led the Habitat for Humanity project for her daughter's school for years. In the beginning of their involvement, when Katie was younger, Maureen would make it fun by organizing a sleepover the night before. As Katie grew, they continued to be involved in Habitat, and Katie took on more and more leadership responsibility, culminating with the honor of being selected as the Chair of the Steering Committee for Habitat in her senior year of high school. She had learned how to run an organization as well as many practical carpentry skills. Volunteering was a special time for Maureen and Katie to be together, so it was always a positive experience.

When asked why volunteering was so gratifying to her, Katie's response was, "Because through Habitat you are providing a house for someone." When asked why she continued to volunteer even after Katie graduated from high school, Maureen says, "The thing I most enjoy is seeing the kids grow and mature. They learn how to work with people, how to organize, how to build a house and a practical way of caring for others."

The best proof of this positive influence in Katie's life is the fact that as a college student, she has continued to volunteer and give her time generously. Katie is a well-known figure on her campus, as she keeps "Richie," a big, white labradoodle, with her at all times as a part of his training in an organization that trains dogs for handicapped people. This requires extensive preparation and guidance as well as an eighteen-month commitment. At the end of this time, Katie will give her puppy up to his new owner. "Richie" will help make a difference in the life of a handicapped person as a guide dog and companion.

Asked what was most significant about their shared volunteer time together, Maureen says, "I think I've done a good job; the biggest thing is, you do it as a family and you make it a priority." Some people may say, 'Well, I don't know if my child wants me to be up there.' You know, you don't have to be hammering side by side, but in the car ride home, you talk about it and it's a time of sharing. The more you spend that time with your kid, the more you have something to share and talk about, which allows you to have open communication about other things. The feeling of self-worth that your child gets from doing and giving to other people builds self-confidence. I'm very proud of Katie."

Generous Kids Quotes

"In church I gave $40 and it helped out a relief effort in Africa, but it really made a difference in me because I was not feeling too good, then I gave and I felt great."

Bruce—age 16

"Once I gave a Pokemon card to Tom. It made a difference because it is Tom's favorite Pokemon!"

Warren—age 7

"My friend lost her dad. It was a really hard time for her and her mom. I went over there every day to comfort them through their loss."

Christina—age 15

*"Giving means you offer something to
people from your heart."*

LJ—age 13

*"I gave a friend of mine my time, and it made a difference in her
life. I think often, people think that giving incorporates an object,
but all my friend needed was a friend's support and a shoulder
to cry on for a few hours."*

Nina—age 20

*"Giving to someone is about showing how you feel about the
person you give to. It's about love and compassion."*

Elsie—age 16

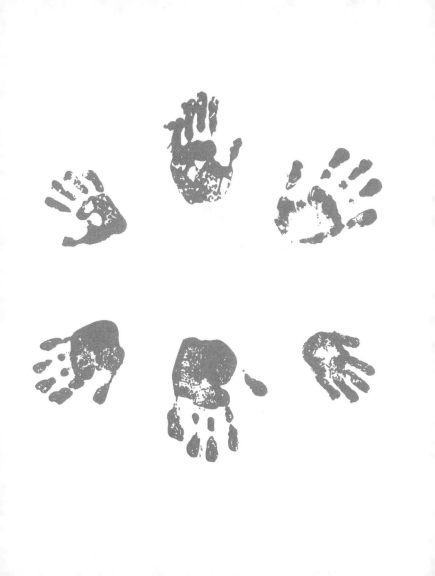

Chapter Thirty-One

Community Service
Three-Step

"Your living is determined not so much by what life brings to you as by what you bring to life."

—*John Homer Miller*

These are the kinds of statements you will hear from kids who participated in giving or volunteering *but didn't get to see the results of their generosity:*

"We collected 232 cans of food, but why?"

"The hallways of our school were filled with clothes, canned goods, cleaning supplies. They all left in a truck. I guess all that stuff helped some people."

"Sorting clothes in the back room of the re-sale store is boring. What I want to know is, what's happening out front? Who are those people?"

What's even worse than a kid not giving? A child who engages in giving but then concludes that it didn't make a difference.

Many high school students who put in mandatory "community service" hours end up feeling like, "What's the big deal?" "Who cares?" "Why do I even do this?" This attitude develops because kids, and all human beings in fact, desire to see the connection between effort and outcome. *We want to connect what we are doing with the people we are helping.*

One of the key things we learned from the student's answers to our "Giving Project" questionnaire is that **kids of all ages need to see "the fruits of their labor"** especially when they are first learning to make giving a habit.

For children ages ten and up, community service is a wonderful way to instill the habit of giving. Be aware that when you put community service into your personal or educational curriculum, you want to be sure to do the "Community Service Three-Step!"

Step #1: *Let them determine what the service will be.*

You will help your kids or students maximize both their effort and enjoyment when you allow them to choose between several worthy options—or bring one of their own ideas to the party.

Allowing such options gives young people ownership in their giving, a fact that is especially important as kids get older.

Encourage them to be honest about what they want from volunteering. By encouraging them to think **intentionally** about what they want from these gifts of their **time, talent, and treasure,** you will provide a much greater chance that their experience will be positive instead of drudgery.

Here are some points to consider:

- ◆ Who and/or where to serve

  - Toddlers

  - Elementary ages or schools

  - Special needs children

  - Adults

- Seniors

- Animals

- Environmental needs

♦ Type of service/why do we want to do this?

  - Making something (Habitat for Humanity, building benches for seniors, helping with a Scout project)

  - Collecting something (food, clothes, toys, toothbrushes)

  - Serving (candy striper at local hospital, tutoring students, playing games with kids)

  - Fundraising (almost every organization needs help raising money)

Step #2: *Let the kids take the lead!*

Expect them to make mistakes—they will. It's part of the learning process. Be there to guide them along the way, not to do it for them. Resist the temptation to "jump in" and take over. Help them learn the process of organizing and giving something to others. Once you and your child or group have decided on what your area of service will be, try this outline to move forward (allow them to "tweak" this outline to fit the service).

- Research the area of interest
    - Focus on a specific problem or need
    - Get the facts
- Brainstorm ways you can help in this area
    - Do you want to
        - Make something
        - Collect something
        - Serve
        - Raise money

- ◆ Create an action plan

  - Contact organizations that work in the area you want to help

  - Find out what they need in terms of making, collecting, serving, or raising funds

  - Decide where to contribute

  - Put together an action plan with a calendar

  - If working in a group, decide who will do what and by when

- ◆ Begin!

You'll be amazed at what happens in the process. The giving will become kid-generated instead of adult-mandated.

Step #3: *Make sure they find out about the people they have helped.*

This third step is powerful, for when young people experience direct involvement with the people they are helping, their giving goes straight to their heart, whether through coaching a Special Olympics child, passing out food at the homeless shelter, or making necklaces with the seniors. Such positive experiences occur because there is a direct relationship between their action and the outcome.

Making this necessary connection becomes more challenging when students are involved in indirect giving such as raising money, building a playground, making a walking path, doing a marathon event for an organization, selling at a resale store that benefits the poor, creating and distributing pamphlets about conserving energy, etc. This type of giving is still VERY important, but when your child is involved indirectly, it's even more necessary for the results to be reported. Their hearts still need to be touched!

When direct contacts are not available, have them ask the organization they supported to send pictures, video footage, letters from the recipients, or whatever else will show the effect their giving has had. Kids "get" giving when they see the results.

And parents, even if your child's high school does not require community service hours, you can!!!

Generous Kids know their giving makes an impact in others' lives. They have LEARNED the habit!

Chapter Thirty-Two

Additional Resources

For a more-complete listing of organizations check out:

Students in Service to America

National Service Learning Clearinghouse

Remember always to check out an organization for yourself. An excellent Web site that rates charities in terms of fiscal responsibility is

Charity Navigator
1200 MacArthur Boulevard
Second Floor
Mahwah, NJ 07430
201.818.1288
http://www.charitynavigator.org

Resources:

America's Promise—The Alliance for Youth
909 N. Washington Street #400
Alexandria, VA 22314-1556
703.684.4500
http://www.americaspromise.org

Boys & Girls Clubs of America
National Headquarters
1275 Peachtree Street N. E.
Atlanta, GA 30309
404.487.5700
http://www.bcga.org

Boy Scouts of America
1325 West Walnut Hill Lane
P. O. Box 152079
Irving, TX 75038-3008
972.580.2000
http://www.scouting.org

Character Education Partnership
1025 Connecticut Avenue, N.W.
Suite 1011
Washington, DC 20036
800.988.8081
http://www.character.org

The Giraffe Project
197 Second Street
P. O. Box 759
Langley, WA 98260
360.221.7989
http://www.giraffe.org

Girl Scouts of the USA
420 Fifth Avenue
New York, NY 10018-2729
212.852.8000
http://www.girlscouts.org

Good Character.com
Live Wire Media
273 Ninth Street
San Francisco, CA 94103
800.359.KIDS
http://www.goodcharacter.com

Heifer International
1 World Avenue
Little Rock, AR 72201
800.422.0474
http://www.heifer.org

Kids Care Clubs
975 Boston Post Road
Darien, CT 06820
203.656.8052
http://www.kidscare.org

Learn and Serve America
National Service Learning Clearinghouse
ETR Associates
4 Carbonero Way
Scotts Valley, CA 95066
866.245.7378
http://www.servicelearning.org

MercyCorps
3015 SW First Avenue
Portland, OR 97201
800.292.3355
http://www.mercycorps.org

National Wildlife Federation
11100 Wildlife Center Drive
Reston, VA 20190
800.822.9919
http://www.nwf.org

National Youth Leadership Council
1910 West County Road B
St. Paul, MN 55113
651.631.3672
http://www.nylc.org

Network for Good
7920 Norfolk Avenue
Suite 520
Bethesda, MD 20814
866.650.4636
http://www.networkforgood.org

OxfamAmerica
226 Causeway Street
Fifth Floor
Boston, MA 02114
800.776.9326
http://www.oxfamamerica.org

The Points of Light Foundation, Youth & Family Outreach
1400 I Street, NW, Suite 800
Washington, DC 20005
202.729.8135
http://www.pointsoflight.org

Youth Service America
1101 15th Street NW, Suite 200
Washington, DC 20005-5002
202.296.2992
http://www.ysa.org/nysd/resources.html

World Vision
P.O. Box 78481
Tacoma, WA 98481
888.511.6548
http://www.worldvision.org

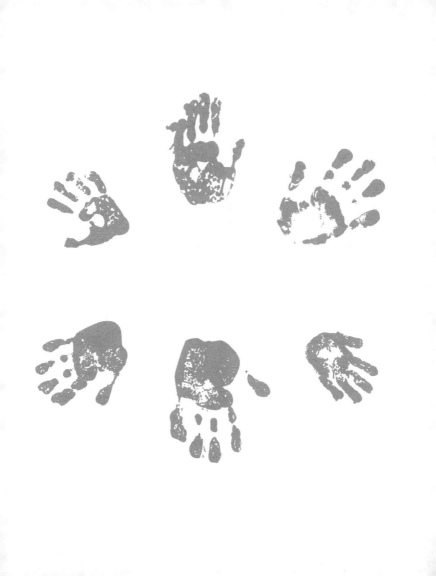

Appendix

"If from infancy you treat children as gods they are liable in adulthood to act as devils."

—*P. D. James*

Seven Ways to Grow a Selfish Kid

As important as it is to know how to raise a generous kid, it is just as important to know some guaranteed ways to ensure that your child turns out selfish:

1. *Let your daughter know that the universe revolves around her!*

   You can accomplish this in several ways: Allow her to be picky about her food. Act like it is cute when she misbehaves in public. Apologize when you have to say "no" to her. Ask for her permission to be in charge. Give her every new gadget known to man. Never insist that she earn her own money.

2. *Have your son wait until he is "ready" to give.*

   Tell him how special (and unusual) it is for him to take the time to give. Remind him that "giving" will look good on his résumé and might guarantee him a spot at an Ivy League school.

3. *Insist that your children give to **your** favorite charity.*

   Convince your kids that **your** cause should resonate with their consciences. Do their thinking for them and then do your giving through them.

4. *Nag your children about volunteering.*

   Compare them unfavorably with their cousins or neighbors who volunteer more frequently.

5. *Drop your kids off at Habitat for Humanity . . .*

   Then drive to the coffee shop for your Saturday morning latte.

6. *Make sure your son never experiences the consequences of his mistakes.*

   This way you will protect him . . . from maturity.

7. *Always assume that your child is blameless.*

   In any conflict with outside authority, defend your kid. Make him or her immune to any and all criticism—even constructive criticism.

Voilà! One selfish kid!!

Acknowledgments

There were so many people who helped us along the way we could never mention them all. Please forgive any oversight. We appreciate everyone who has supported *Generous Kids*.

We are especially grateful to the following:

Dale Godby, PhD, Zig Ziglar, Dan Sullivan and Babs Smith, David Bach, Erin Jamieson, Lauren Roberts and William Storey, Adam Christing, Mark Woods, Tom Pruit, PhD, Richard Rossi, Debra and Nick Schatzki, Jennifer Bhatthal, David Brown, Gail and David Cook, Teresa Easler, Billy Grammer, Samara Kline, Jeff Crilley, Maureen McClelland, Cyndi Bassel, Gretchen Montgomery, Joe Christensen, and Nancy Koop.

All the teachers who helped with the questionnaire and especially the kids whose answers motivated us to write this book, everyone at Brown Books, everyone at Strategic Coach, and our clients.

All our family and friends who helped us in so many ways!!

A special thank-you to our boys Jonathan, Stephen, and Addison, who continue to inspire us and keep our lives interesting!

About the Authors

> "There is a wonderful mythical law of nature that the three things we crave most in life —happiness, freedom, and peace of mind— are always attained by giving them to someone else."

> —*Peyton Conway March*

Meet Colleen O'Donnell and Lyn Baker, single moms who have raised three generous (most of the time) sons. Colleen and Lyn share a passion for helping kids "get it" about giving. Their combined experiences as parents, teachers, volunteers, scout leaders, tutors, administrators, and mentors have allowed them to influence hundreds of kids of all ages. Lyn and Colleen want to share with other parents these simple tools so they can teach their children the habit of giving.

Colleen O'Donnell has been a successful business owner for over fifteen years. She is an exciting and sought after presenter who speaks nationwide on the topics of financial planning and balancing work and home life. Colleen invests her time and resources in her community, church, and her son's school. Her clients enjoy her love of life as much as her expertise.

Lyn Baker earned her master's degree from SUNY and has worked in education for twenty years. She is a charismatic teacher, writer, playwright, and director and has worked with students from preschool through college age. As an administrator in three private schools, she has observed firsthand the difference generosity makes in a child's life.

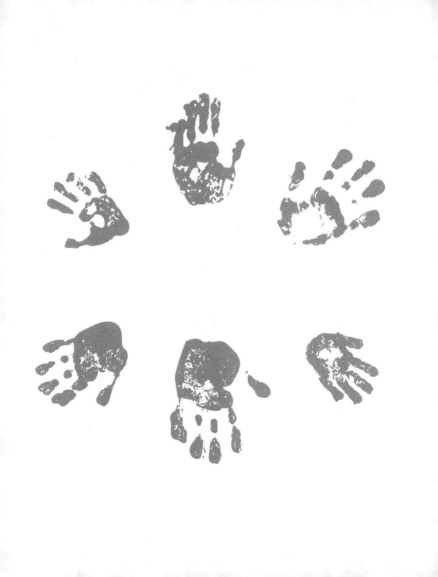

End Notes

1.   UCLA/Higher Education Research Institute, 1991.

2.   Search Institute, 1995.

3.   Independent Sector/Gallup 1996.

4.   http://www.independentsector.org

5.   *Youth Helping America* fact sheet, Corporation for National and Community Service

6.   *Giving USA 2006*, AAFRC Trust for Philanthropy

7.   *Youth Helping America* fact sheet, Corporation for National and Community Service

8.   http://www.nationalservice.gov

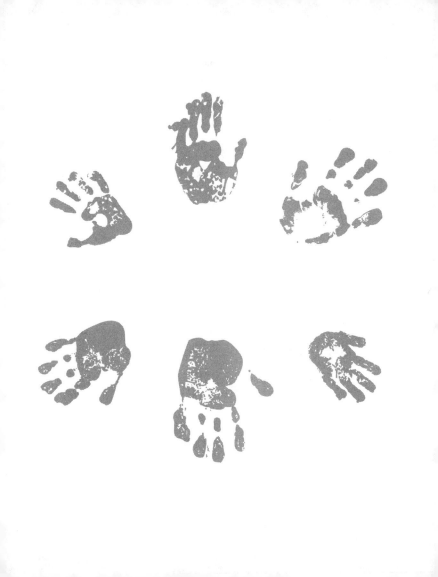